PATIENCE

BY MARI SCHUH

BLUE OWL
BOOKS

TIPS FOR CAREGIVERS

Social and emotional learning (SEL) helps children connect with their emotions and gain a better understanding of themselves. Mindfulness can support this learning and help them develop a kind and inclusive mentality. By incorporating mindfulness and SEL into early learning, students can establish this mentality early and be better equipped to build strong connections and communities.

BEFORE READING

Talk to the student about patience.

Discuss: What does patience mean to you? Talk about a time you were very patient. Did being patient help you? Did it help others?

AFTER READING

Talk to the student about practicing patience.

Discuss: How can being patient make you a better friend? How do you feel when someone is not patient with you? How can you be more patient with yourself?

SEL GOAL

Brainstorm with students about ways they can be patient at home and at school. Be sure to include situations in which they can be patient with themselves. Review their ideas. Find similarities and differences in the examples. Ask students what they learned. When can they be more patient?

TABLE OF CONTENTS

CHAPTER 1
What Is Patience?...4

CHAPTER 2
Patience Every Day..8

CHAPTER 3
Patience with Yourself...................................16

GOALS AND TOOLS
Grow with Goals...22
Mindfulness Exercise....................................22
Glossary...23
To Learn More..23
Index...24

WHAT IS PATIENCE?

Carter's birthday party is today! He is excited to open his gifts, but he needs to wait. Some of his friends are not at the party yet.

Carter is calm and doesn't get upset. He is **patient**. He knows that opening gifts will be fun whenever it happens!

Patience is being calm while you wait. It also means understanding if things don't go the way you want them to.

Leo is ready to go to the park. But his little sister isn't ready yet. Leo is calm. He kindly helps her.

CHAPTER 2

PATIENCE EVERY DAY

You can be patient every day. Patience isn't just for people. You can also be patient with things. Blair's tablet isn't working. At first, she is upset. She almost hits her tablet.

But Blair chooses to be patient. She is **mindful**. She checks in with her **emotions** and takes deep breaths. This helps her calm down.

Ben is patient at school. He raises his hand in class. He calmly waits for his teacher to call on him.

At lunch, Ben waits in line. He is really hungry, but he doesn't cut in line. He makes a new friend while he waits.

Relationships are better when people are patient. When you are patient with your friends, you are a good friend. People enjoy spending time with you.

Being patient is a way to be kind, too. Joe's uncle tells a long story. Joe has already heard this story, but he smiles and listens to it again. He doesn't want to hurt his uncle's feelings.

HAVING EMPATHY

Patience helps us have **empathy**. It helps us **accept** other people as they are. It can help us understand the challenges people are facing.

Being in a hurry can make people **impatient**. People who are impatient might get mad or disappointed. If you feel this way, try to slow down. Take time to be present and mindful. Cook with an adult. Make a craft. Read a book. These things take time. They can help you be a patient person.

USING MINDFULNESS

When you feel impatient, try to **focus** on your breathing. Take a few slow, deep breaths. Be mindful of how you feel in the moment. This will help you practice patience.

PATIENCE WITH YOURSELF

It is important to be patient with yourself, too. Nina broke her arm. She can't play basketball. She has to be patient while it heals. If she plays with a broken arm, she could hurt it worse!

Learning new skills takes patience. Rani is learning how to draw. She knows it will take time to learn. She practices each day and looks back at her **progress**.

Tiana just started soccer. She is patient with herself while she learns and practices. She gets better slowly. After months of practice, she scores the winning goal in the big game!

Patience is an important part of being happy and successful. It can help you focus on and **achieve** your **goals**.

PRACTICE IT

Set a timer. Write the alphabet backward from Z to A. How long did it take you? Try again. Can you beat your record? Each time gets easier. Do you notice your patience working?

It can be hard to wait. Everyone gets upset and impatient sometimes. That's OK. Patience is a skill. Keep practicing it. How? Be mindful. Think about your feelings. Try to understand why you need to wait. Be positive!

WHILE YOU WAIT

Try talking to the person next to you while waiting in line. If you still feel impatient, try naming three things you see, hear, or feel. The wait won't seem as long!

GOALS AND TOOLS

GROW WITH GOALS

It's not always easy to be patient. We can become more patient with practice and by being mindful of our emotions.

Goal: Learning a new hobby or sport can take time. Think of new things you would like to learn. How can you stay patient as you learn something new?

Goal: Think about a time when someone was helpful and patient with you. What did they do? How can you do that for others?

Goal: How can you be more patient at home and at school? Write down your ideas. Think about these goals the next time you start to feel impatient.

MINDFULNESS EXERCISE

Being mindful of how you feel can help you be patient. Follow these steps to keep yourself from getting upset and impatient.

1. Notice how you are feeling right now. Take time to notice how your whole body feels. How do you feel? What are you thinking about?

2. Take deep, slow breaths. Closely watch your stomach slowly go in and out.

3. Remind yourself that you can't control what is happening. But you can control how you act.

4. Try to understand what is going on. Be positive and hopeful. Aim to act in a kind way.

GLOSSARY

accept
To agree that something is correct, satisfactory, or enough.

achieve
To do something successfully after making an effort.

emotions
Feelings, such as happiness, sadness, or anger.

empathy
The ability to understand and be sensitive to the thoughts and feelings of others.

focus
To concentrate on something.

goals
Things you aim to do.

impatient
Unable to put up with problems or delays without getting angry or upset.

mindful
A mentality achieved by focusing on the present moment and calmly recognizing and accepting your feelings, thoughts, and sensations.

patient
Able to put up with problems or delays without getting angry or upset.

progress
Forward movement or improvement.

relationships
The ways in which people feel about and behave toward one another, or the ways in which two or more people are connected.

TO LEARN MORE

FACT SURFER

Finding more information is as easy as 1, 2, 3.

1. Go to www.factsurfer.com

2. Enter "**patience**" into the search box.

3. Choose your cover to see a list of websites.

INDEX

breaths 9, 15

calm 5, 7, 9, 11

disappointed 15

emotions 9

empathy 12

excited 4

friends 4, 11, 12

goals 19

helps 7, 9, 12, 15, 19

impatient 15, 20

kind 12

learning 17, 19

line 11, 20

listens 12

mad 15

mindful 9, 15, 20

practice 15, 17, 19, 20

relationships 12

school 11

skills 17, 20

tablet 8

teacher 11

upset 5, 8, 20

wait 4, 7, 11, 20

Blue Owl Books are published by Jump!, 5357 Penn Avenue South, Minneapolis, MN 55419, www.jumplibrary.com

Copyright © 2021 Jump! International copyright reserved in all countries. No part of this book may be reproduced in any form without written permission from the publisher.

Library of Congress Cataloging-in-Publication Data

Names: Schuh, Mari C., 1975– author.
Title: Patience / by Mari Schuh.
Description: Blue Owl books. | Minneapolis: Jump!, Inc., 2021. | Series: Mindful mentality | Includes index.
Audience: Ages 7–10 | Audience: Grades 2–3
Identifiers: LCCN 2019059974 (print)
LCCN 2019059975 (ebook)
ISBN 9781645273837 (library binding)
ISBN 9781645273844 (paperback)
ISBN 9781645273851 (ebook)
Subjects: LCSH: Patience—Juvenile literature.
Classification: LCC BJ1533.P3 S39 2021 (print)
LCC BJ1533.P3 (ebook) | DDC 179/.9—dc23
LC record available at https://lccn.loc.gov/2019059974
LC ebook record available at https://lccn.loc.gov/2019059975

Editor: Jenna Gleisner
Designer: Molly Ballanger

Photo Credits: Darrin Henry/Shutterstock, cover; Viktoriia Likhonosova/Shutterstock, 1; Sergey Novikov/Shutterstock, 3; Lopolo/Shutterstock, 4, 5; kwanchaichaiudom/Getty, 6–7; Prostock-Studio/iStock, 8, 9; Comstock Images/Getty, 10–11; Diego Cervo/Shutterstock, 12–13; bearinmind/Shutterstock, 14–15; FatCamera/iStock, 16; Peter Mason/Cultura Limited/SuperStock, 17; John Giustina/Getty, 18–19; joSon/Getty, 20–21.

Printed in the United States of America at Corporate Graphics in North Mankato, Minnesota.